New Orleans
BETWEEN POETRY AND THE BLUES

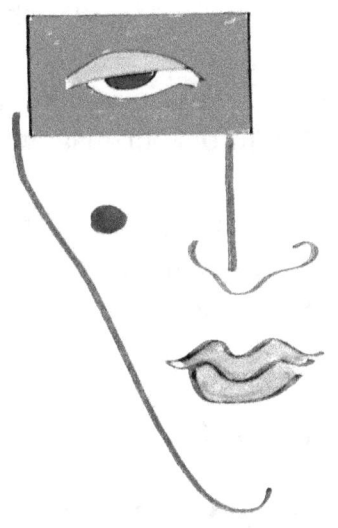

PHYLLIS B. PARUN

Copyright © 2019 PHYLLIS B. PARUN

All Rights Reserved. No part of this publication may be reproduced or transmitted in any means, electronic or mechanical, including photocopying, recording, or any information storage and retrieval system, without permission in writing. For permissions contact the publisher or author.

Cover art and all illustrations are solely owned by the author and requires permissions.

Permission to make copies of any part of this work can be submitted in email to
pbpstudio@yahoo.com

Cover Design by Phyllis Parun
ISBN: 978-1-7323560-3-0

BERNARD PRESS
Publisher
New Orleans, Louisiana

Inaugural Edition

Dedicated to
Bernard Parun Jr.,
my loyal brother and friend
for seven decades.

CONTENTS

Flood Water, 1
Life, 9
Zulu Times, 11
Mardi Gras Loot, 13
Life of New Orleans Poet, 15
White Linen, 17
Grandmothers House, 19
The Visit, 21
Collateral Damage, 23
Sounds, 27
Southern Decadence, 29
Face, 31
Symphony Night, 33
The Art of the Brush, 35
Spring, 37
New Orleans My Home, 39
Time, 49
The Last Time, 51
That's a Nice Tomb, 53
Tears, 55
Clouds, 57
Decades, 59
Are we Free Yet? 61
Bad Hair, 65
Slavery, 67
Epitaph, 69
Humans, 71
Greek TV, 73
When, 75
Lines, 77
City Park, 79
Memories, 81
Thursday. 83
Fronds. 85
Still Full of Youth. 87

Acknowledgments, 89
Author Biography, 92
End Notes, 93

FLOOD WATER FLOOD WATER

       1

New Orleans never was the kind of city
anyone could tame or capture.
She always had her own mystique.
Outwardly, though she appeared
      hospitable and inviting, inwardly she had
      a secretive and private nature.
Sought after by rich and poor alike,
with a reputation for frivolity that circled the globe,
      she remained humble and silent
about what was closest to her heart.

       2

Rearranged by lake waters,
now she is a city in ruins.
The home we knew and nurtured, destroyed,
      her buildings washed into the ground,
      her people sent into exile,
and even though media giants combed her streets
blasting news of horror and rubble to the world,
      they never found our real New Orleans.
They simply did not know where to look.

3

In New Orleans nothing
was ever quite as it appeared.
A city of masks and masquerades,
a spiritual Mecca to whom pilgrims flocked
> for cures from social ills
> > and relief from political repression
She was a healer, a cleanser of souls,
with a talent for comic relief,
she infuses new life into tired and worn ones.
Thought to reside along the Mississippi,
she is and remains a Brigadoon.

4

New Orleans is old, very old.
New Orleanians live with and love old things.
We live in old houses,
> collect old objects, wear old clothes,
> > and drive old cars. We do not much like
participating in consumerism.
Trash picking is our favorite past time,
making art out of found objects is our business.
Furnishing our homes in New Orleans eclectic is
our style.

Cheap rent and a low cost of living
perfected our art of living
comfortably below the poverty line,
We, New Orleanians lived life
on the edge of everything.

5
At the end of the mighty Mississippi River,
where sixty thousand chemicals of waste flows
into her drinking water daily,
New Orleans is this country's industrial dumping
    ground, heating up the Gulf,
    killing life and wetlands.
Hated by conservatives
who could not conquer her spirit,
New Orleans has and remains
    a political battleground.
With centuries of tempered defiant bravado,
she has successfully resisted large corporate
takeovers and the installation of
a factory economy.

6

New Orleans has never been homogenized.
From her very beginnings
a ragtag, renegade population
of French, German, Irish, Spanish, settled here.
Her builders and residents were black, white,
    rich and poor, living side by side
    in "salt and pepper" neighborhoods
    set the tone for a unique social mix.
More like a small neighborhood than a city,
    her houses were hand built
    her culture homegrown.
Black people from neighboring towns
flocked to her for refuge.
With a majority African-American population,
New Orleans before the storm was
just about as close to a third world country
as you could find in the USA.

7

Before the storm New Orleans was
a city of artists, dreamers, and visionaries
    where cultural freedom thrived
      and being eccentric was de rigueur.
She was a land where creativity
oozed out of the ground,
songs spilled out of houses and
car doors onto her streets.
Every culture within her borders
thrived on her inspiration.
Economically her industry was tourism,
and she was never 100%
given over to wealth or possessions.
Before the waters of Katrina flooded her,
    the streets of New Orleans
    were flooded with a diverse
and vibrant cultural life.

8
New Orleans was not a city of money.
    What she had were deep roots -
    deep national, racial, economic,
family and community ties.
She was never part of
what mainstream USA was about.
She was simply a fun-loving town inhabited
by ingenious culturally rich folks.

9
When Katrina's waters rose and
the massive Diaspora began
New Orleanians were thrust from our cocoon
    into an alien land -
    and without our costumes.
The media did not see us at all.
What the media looked for was
    skin color and money.
What the media wrote was that our people were poor.

10

The media called us poor because
>we lived on their poverty line.

They called us poor because we did not
partake in the luxury and consumer culture.
They called us poor because we had
>a handmade culture.

They called us poor because we
>created our own dreams.

They called us poor because we did not
>embrace their corporate domination.

They called us poor because we were
a shopkeeper economy.

What they did not write about was
>that we are a people who value our culture,

our families, our friends and our community
more than money.
What they did write about was
>their own racism and poverty of spirit.

What they did not write about was
what prosperity really is.

11

Instead, all they wrote about was money.
They never saw our people
They never heard our many voices.
They never saw the heart and soul of New Orleans.
They never recognized
our simple gift to the world.

12

Amongst the noise of all their corporate media frenzy
they highlighted the essential question that
the waters of Katrina raised.
They delivered one single, minded message
loud and clear:
How truly impoverished and dehumanized
The most powerful and wealthiest country
on the globe really is.
And the people of the world heard them,
loud and clear.

~

It is the nature of life
to exist only for a moment.

~

FROM THE ZULU TIMES

Early in its New Orleans history
Zulu walked.
Zulu walked down Claiborne Avenue
as peasantry.

Today Zulu rides
on floats across the Mississippi River
following Rex
down St. Charles Avenue
as royalty.

~

MARDI GRAS LOOT

Mardi Gras
Everywhere.
Beads
Throughout the house
On every neck,
Loot abounds.

Go out and catch you some.

And see a parade
Every night
Three times on a weekend, if you like.

Loot, Loot, Loot!
See kids stepping on hands
Pushing you aside
For loot.

~

LIFE OF A NEW ORLEANS POET

First there was poetry, descriptive images,
beautifully crafted vivid lines,
sonorous lyrics and angry rants.
Then there was coffee, imported, dark, roasted,
black, *cafe au lait*, bitter and sweet coffee.
Then there was poetry in coffeehouses,
lyrical, vivid, poignant lines
with dark brews and witty friends.
Then there was poetry in bars, dark, dingy,
cigarette-filled-alcohol-stinking bars
poetry accompanied by booze, slurred phrases,
blurry eyes and days of drunken memory loss.
Finally there was only the alcohol.

WHITE LINEN

The drunkards
    the drugged
    the anesthetized
    and the addicted
The sick
    the diseased
    and the dying
The bored
    the frustrated
    all dressed in white
    roaming the streets
    looking pretty
viewing exhibits
    censoring the voices of freedom
    deadening the senses.
One could die from having one's spirit killed
    on this one night alone
Or one could kill oneself in protest
    and maybe get mentioned
    as a one liner in a major newspaper
and maybe your cause would be revealed -
    maybe, if you were lucky -

and then a month later
    everyone would forget all about you
and your artistic expression
    or maybe they'd psychoanalyze you
and your cause out of existence
and you'd be dead to the public.

Then they'd just go on
    with their bourgeois lives
    painting everything pretty again
    renovating the truths
    and the sorrows
so they can't be found - anywhere - anymore
until the next protesting, hurting, frustrated
    soul explodes on the scene
painting truths and repeating the cycle
yet again.

White Linen -
Deadened people
making nice
of everything.

~

GRANDMOTHER'S HOUSE

This ancestral home
the scent of three generations
linger - still

Aunt Mary, there
in her patio garden - cultivating poinsettias
Uncle Peter - at his oak desk
studying accounting
Grandmother - at the cooking pot
making oyster stew -
It smells like home

And now
my brother's photograph
still on the round oak family table
where he once ate now an altar
his ashes in the parlor
where his bed once stood.

This dying place
grandfather, grandmother, aunt,
and brother   all -
passed on - here.

Memories live here now

When sold
the nouveaux riche
would gut these plaster walls to the studs -
modern conquistadors
stripping decades of immigrant life
substituting sheetrock, pop culture,
and gentrification -
all doomed to the short life
and the death due them
as so much trash from post-industrial civilization
a mere parody of its former self.

Grandmother's house
ancestral home
place of love and wisdom
now a relic of cultural memory
slated for erasure
in this era of deletions.

- I lament.

~

THE VISIT

A visit with old friends
At the Museum
        Works of art.

~

COLLATERAL DAMAGE:
Goodbye Don't Ask Don't Tell

Growing up in
the dark ages of the 1950's
when you were my first love   and I was yours
your life came crashing down   around me
when your parents   and mine
wanted us married
when modern psychiatry used
death drugs, shock therapy, lobotomies
and homophobic propaganda trying to
change us into heterosexuals   because
loving our own sex   was a disease
back then.
            Goodbye DADT

In spite of these assaults
we loved right through   the darkness
the marriages and the birth of children
the homophobia
the liberation wars
fighting for freedom   our freedom
to love each other
through all the years
of oppression and patronization

the story of our love told
in "The Children's Hour"
and "Therese and Isabelle"
right down to "The Kids are Alright".
     Goodbye DADT

Still we can never forget   the days when we could not
kiss or hold hands in public   or
take our lover home for family holidays
being in the closet at work   and overly cautious
when looking for apartments to live in   together;
we can never forget the anguish of denial
and looking the other way
when anti-gay jokes   were told right in front of us.
     Goodbye DADT

Now after many years of alienation   we
still carry around scars   as honor badges
for the choices we made long ago
in the darkness when we were young
and it was our fate to drive deep into the
patriarchy without each other
our wounds not yet healed.

Are we free to write our own futures
free to live our own truths
free from our fears?
Have we finally driven
through the darkness   and
are we now out on the other side?
　　Goodbye DADT

~

SOUNDS

Sounds of poetry
Linger in the morning air
      A foggy mist.

~

SOUTHERN DECADENCE

This September morn
trashy faggots
dressed in second hand clothes
strutting their imitation stuff
up and down Frenchman Street
in this City of Fantasies.
There ain't nothin' "straight"
about this day of Decadence
except the Bar and drug dealers'
9am Tuesday morning drive
to the Bank.

It's a cornucopia of fantasies
in a sea of humanity
playing out everyone's
wildest dreams.
Smut everywhere,
drugs, alcohol, sexual acting out
and simply down and dirty sleaze.

~

FACE

Personal road
Pathway back
 The Face.

~

SYMPHONY NIGHT

An empty house
lays waiting in anticipation.
A walk through the Fairmont -
hotel of my childhood.
Standing before the Blue Room Door closed now
where my family and I
would dine and dance in the 50's.
Streets filled with visitors
Itzak Perlman playing violin at the Orpheum
while I, standing across the street
feeling one with the staff hanging around out front
dressed in my symphony usher's best
while they in their working best
stand in drizzling rain,
cabs gathering, umbrella's bobbing.
And I, like the bag lady on the bench,
slipping through the cracks of society, reminisce.
This was and is my life.

Sitting in the borrowed car
"Park Here" staring at me from the lot -
Hundreds of people
piling out of the theatre
mere forms floating through space.
I feel nothing
Odd couples go to and fro
leaving me wondering
how they ever matched up.

~

THE ART OF THE BRUSH

One day a student approached her teacher
asking what is the secret of drawing
with sumi brush on handmade paper.
The teacher gave her this
traditional instruction:
"Fast for four days and empty yourself
of all concerns."

The student laughed and asked again
the secret of drawing with sumi brush on
handmade paper
It seems she feared ruining the paper.
This time the teacher's instructions were:
"Take deep breaths. Contemplate the truth
that there are no mistakes, that things can only
happen once and your brush will execute your
breath."

Days later the student approached
the teacher once again
this time reporting that she
could not fast for four days,
and commenting that surely
this must have been some sort of joke
then asking the teacher
how to approach the handmade paper
which she feared she would ruin.
This time the teacher's final instructions were:

"Do not be afraid of spontaneity.
Choose the most beautiful paper you can find,
take a deep breath concentrate
all of your energy on the paper
with your brush and draw."

~

SPRING

It's night
Birds sing outside my window
      Spring dawns.

~

NEW ORLEANS, MY HOME

New Orleans, my home.
My home, my home, my home.
The place of my birth
family tombs
failed dreams
dashed fame
and lost love.

New Orleans, my home --
Who are you who persists in my consciousness?
Why have I not gone from you years ago,
left, along with my classmates for greener
pastures when I was young
and there was still time and a future?
You and I are like a bad marriage,
persisting through it all
so much that I love
so much that I don't
so many years
of entanglements.

New Orleans, my birthplace --
origin of my dreams,
window to the world
myriad cultures parading by
an entire city living in the past
with no future to speak of.
53 years of travel
in this one place
looking out of this one window
watching this universe of multi-cultures
and ethnic tribes come and go
talking not of Michelangelo
but of fame, wealth and failed dreams.

Five decades
of technology and social changes
from ice boxes to radios - that's the pre-TV Era
(yes, Virginia there was such a time)
and no AC in houses or autos
(even in this Southern heat).

I have been here -
riding the city bus to school with a sign that read
"Whites Only" staring me in the face -
through the Mississippi civil rights marches
and white flight,
through NASA and Sputnik,
through the Kennedy assassination
and Attorney General Jim Garrison's investigation,
through the Beatnik coffee houses
and poetry readings,
through the Hippies' pot and acid.
women's lib, gay lib, leftist Marxism
and the Vinceremos Brigade;
through J. Edgar "Mary" Hoover's FBI spies
and all of his files
through the opening of China
and Nixon's resignation
I have been in this New Orleans,
city of contrasts and reversals
my high school not one Black in 1959
not one white in 1995.
Born a Christian now a Taoist -
It's half a century later.

New Orleans, a city of parades
parades
parades
parades – parades!
Parades of Mardi Gras
parades of jazz funerals
any excuse parades
parading past my window
Doo op
rock and roll
progressive jazz
and that is all that has progressed
in this antique city.
We have it all
and I have missed none of it.

And festivals
Festivals
FESTIVALS!
Festivals for jazz
Festivals for Bastille Day
for crawfish
for tomatoes
for decadence
for dogs and roaches.
Yes, even roaches.

Half a century of parades
parading past my window.
My entire life experience
all rolled up into this one place.

A city of cemeteries -
death and life side by side
so many have died
passing from one existence to another
so much death to mourn
so much sorrow to digest
so much life to celebrate.

New Orleans, my home
of familiar streets and European buildings
memories on every corner
impossible to escape its past
impossible to escape my past.
New Orleans, you entomb my memories,
hanging on the architecture
like so much Spanish moss on 300 year old Oaks.

New Orleans, my home
What are you to me that
I persist here for so many years

through economic depression,
intellectual isolation, aesthetic bankruptcy,
moral depravity, social decadence?
Who are you who occupies
my only time on this planet
with your European beauty
and your African culture?
Why do you persist in my memory?
You, city of murderers, thieves, gamblers,
tourists, unemployed and retired
living side by side with the dead
in this soup of a swamp and I keeping the
company of these lost souls in this Alice in
wonderland of queens and drags
and now our undead rising up into Hollywood
with my brain frying a little each day
in the summer heat and
the vacuity of this coffeehouse society,
few real artists talking aesthetics in the streets
and no philosophers' renaissance
and I, dying a little more each day for some
depth of philosophical conversation.
It's no Paris in the 20's!

New Orleans, looking for its identity.
A city of slogans in a swamp
this Deep South Crescent City
like OL' Man River just keeps rollin' along
"The City that Care Forgot"
forgot to care,
Hollywood in Louisiana
"The Dream State" dreaming of fame
and fortune
"The Other LA"
"The Big Easy" where your Daddy's rich and
your Mama's good lookin' --
You wish!

New Orleans,
home of my inspiration
here where I have been daughter, sister,
student, teacher, organizer, philosopher,
sculptor, and I, who never learned to write the
English language properly
now becoming a poet

53 years
from John McCrady's Art School
to Chinese medical philosophy
now hooked up to Cyberspace
zooming out of this eternal now
into the global universe --
because I'm connected--
connected through this
window of New Orleans.

New Orleans
the anus of the Mississippi -
asshole of this industrial waste of the Delta -
this creative culture that doesn't care
this melting pot that melted
leaving no national borders
this lala land of a Hollywood set
this clown town of the USA
and me just another clown.
This party town USA
music on every corner
and I, who had been mistaken for Stella
by all them damn Yankees my whole life
living on this Desire Street bus line
just a block away from heaven.

New Orleans, my birthplace
home of friends
tombs of ancestors.
My New Orleans
city of dreamers
   and the dreamed.

~

TIME

Tell me, my friend, what is the time?
Is it always now?
Eternal now?

So will there be a later, a tomorrow?
What time will it be then?

Another today?
Another now?

~

THE LAST TIME

When will be the last time
You hear anyone's voice
The last phone call
The last look
The last walk
last smile
last breath
When will that last time be?

～

THAT'S A NICE TOMB

That's a nice tomb!
New Orleans is full of tombs
whole cities for the dead
above ground tombs big as houses
embellished with finely carved
figurative sculpture.

Here the Dead are dead
the living are dead -
walking dead
Everyone here is dead.

Bodies haunting the streets
taking up space
roaming around
looking for meaning
looking for love
looking for sex and drugs
Finding only the walking dead.

Tombs
City of tombs
City of living dead
walking dead
buried dead
reincarnated dead
and I, foolishly looking for a solution
to my heartbreaking sorrow
among these ruins.

~

TEARS

Red eyes
Cheeks wet with tears
   I am forgetting you.

~

CLOUDS

Face
eyes
mouths
noses
lips
and clouds of cheeks
forming faces I know
and faces I don't
friends, relatives, strangers, spirits
from some distant past or future
leaving messages in the sky

~

DECADES

Decades go by and
years come back
first, as a spot on the distant horizon
then moving full figured into view -
memories from that deep within
placed there long ago
when we were young and innocent
of life's inevitabilities

~

ARE WE FREE YET?

Are we free yet?
Did we dream the dream that
we could live in our own houses
immersed in self-discovery
surrounded by myriad objects
documenting our lives
living freely in the joyous pursuit
of our own personal dreams?

Did we dream
that one day
we would not be
held captive by family obligations
shackled by colonization,
imprisoned by patriarchy,
religion or social conditioning?
Are these the goals we imagined for ourselves
as we fought passionately for our civil liberties
when we were younger and
looked life boldly in the face
and said "Yes! Bring it on!"

Have we now bought our freedom?
Did we dream
that one day we would be
free to love anyone,
free to be feminine or masculine
or androgynous,
free to enjoy sex with anyone we choose,
free to marry or be single,
to reproduce or not,
free to acquire or not,
to contribute to causes, help the poor,
feed the hungry
or live in pursuit of our own personal dreams?
Have we now found the secret of happiness?

Did we dream
that one day we would be
free to travel the globe,
free to be productive,
to be pregnant with ideas or not,
to publish or to perish,
to be remembered or leave in utter anonymity

free to be whatever we want to be,
to live a life of our personal design
not to imitate, not to follow
pre-existing philosophies,
free to create a completely original life
- an envious position indeed in a world
where female slavery still flourishes!

Is this the life
generations of female American activists
have fought so hard and so long for?

Are we free now?
Have we ceased to be slaves and servants?
Is this our time, the era
we strived for decades to create?
So I ask you,
are we done yet or
is there even more to come?

As for now, let us dance and sing and
celebrate our liberté!
Tomorrow will come soon enough.

~

BAD HAIR

I had a haircut today
It's a bad haircut
But no one has commented
No one wants to say it's a bad haircut
But it's a bad haircut.
When I am seen out people don't say anything
There is no "Hey you got your hair cut"
Or "Your hair is shorter"
Or "Your hair is the shortest I've ever seen on you"
There is nothing
No one wants to say
"Hey I see you got a bad haircut"
"It's the worst haircut of your life"
Why the silence?
Your saying so won't spoil the mystery.
It's a bad haircut.
We can leave it at that
Or maybe you already have!

~

SLAVERY

What does a slave look like?
Who can say, we are, after all,
born in this imperialist giant.
Who's to say we're blessed?
We, with our designer labels
and consumer roles.
Could we be the cursed,
chattel in our own time?
Who's to say we're better off
than the women of Afghanistan -
we just another kind of civilized slave
wearing a modern Burka.

~

Epitaph

I lived
　　　I loved
　　　　　I left.

～

HUMANS

We live here in this universe of
sun, earth, air and water
thinking that our lives are purposeful
that we exist for some divine end -
Who are we but mere life forms
and peculiar ones at that
thinking arrogantly that in all of nature
we humans are the most important.

~

GREEK TV

Watching a 1940's Greek movie on TV
remembering my Yugoslav Father
knowing that the world
has changed   irreversibly
romanticizing the past
which is all that can be done with it -
anticipating a collective future
of more homogeneity
and less national conflict
We are the 21st century pioneers.

~

WHEN

When I am old
I will make colorful quilts
sculpt and write poetry
I will dance and play
with children, when I am old.
When I am old
I will hear the sounds
of nature and the
songs of birds.
I will see sunsets and sunrises.
I will dream of beautiful palaces and gold light,
when I am old.
When I am old
I will run thru mountains
dance on water
sleep under stars
eat from forests
lay on sunlight
bathe in rivers
swim in gulfs
sail across oceans -
When I am old.

~

LINES

Lines of my own poetry
drift in and out -
lines of others
crowded out by my own voice
pushed aside my entire life.
All those authors read   forgotten!
All the poems, stories, philosophies   forgotten!
Only those that meant the most to me,
only phrases that seemed my own,
only those that drew out my voice
from deep within me
attached themselves.
All others not remembered.
Only my own phrases,
my own voice,
stands large before me now

~

CITY PARK

City Park –
Trees smile
birds are friends
grass gives off sweet nectar
wind cools the summer heat
sun gives a warm caress
squirrels chase each other
around tree trunks -
no need for human distraction
nature is full.
If we humans are just other animals
why expect more?

~

Memories on every corner
  hanging from your architecture
   like so much Spanish moss
    on 300 year old Oaks

~

THURSDAY

Bike ride
thru City Park
Qigong on the lagoon bank
Three beautiful ducks
with green heads
strut their stuff on the fallen pine
we speaking only in gestures   -
as long as mine are gentle and predictable
they keep their distance.

~

Amongst black kelp fronds
Leafy sea dragons frolic
      Pas de Deux.

~

STILL FULL OF YOUTH

Still full of youth
I run eagerly
into the arms of every new found spiritual tradition
seeking solace and truth
but none comes to greet me.
Mother, father, dear aunts—now all going
And I, becoming my own parent.

Still full of youth
I befriend the elders
hoping that I will find
some scrap of evidence
that with long life also comes happiness
but finding none
other than individual variations
on the theme of personal choices
combined with fate.

Still full of youth
I emerge vainglorious
expecting more than
just a good show from this life.

Still full of youth
I get drunk on food
stay up all night
drinking tea and writing poetry
past the sun's rising and
bird songs announcing the dawn.

~

ACKNOWLEDGEMENTS

Special thanks to Karen E. Doby (Dancing Shark Studio) for indispensible technical support with cover and copy editing. And to Gloria Daniels for giving a reader's opinion and being a valuable sounding board.

PHYLLIS PARUN, New Orleans born, artist-philosopher poet, was raised and educated by Louisiana teacher parents from whom she learned the art of living well through art, dance, music and sports, pursued the study of philosophy at Louisiana State University in New Orleans, the University of Pennsylvania and LSU Baton Rouge. While teaching at Dillard University, Ms. Parun received a grant to attend Harvard in the social sciences. Ms. Parun spent a large part of her adult life in the visual arts as arts-activist, initiating the city's first 1% for Arts Ordinance, operating a Fine and Decorative Arts Studio, restoring antiques and reviving the lost gilded arts. As an arts, health and political activist, Ms. Parun has been a catalyst, shaping the unwritten culture of the New Orleans landscape.

Ms. Parun's published genres include interviews, articles, essays, poems, e-zines, art, and photography in a wide variety of local and national publications: The Beachcomber (LSUNO), Alternatives, Contemporary Arts Southeast, Macrobiotics Today, NonCredo, The Rogue, Pulse (AOBTA), American Assn. of Oriental Medicine, MacroNetjournal, Healthways, Bywater Current, Gulf Coast Arts Review, ArtLit, Iris, Qi: Journal of Traditional Eastern Health and Fitness, The New Laurel Review (2001, 2015), The Maple Leaf Rag III (2006), Mending for Memory (2017) and creator of The New Orleans Living Treasurers Award and The New Orleans Avant-Garde ezine.

Ms. Parun's writing is filled with a wealth of many fulfilling life experiences. Ms. Parun is undoubtedly one of New Orleans' native living treasures.

END NOTES

Thank you for reading the second book of New Orleans poems.

And if you enjoyed this please leave a review at Amazon USA
https://www.amazon.com/- /e/B006HX9348

If you like this one you might also enjoy
"New Orleans Born"
And visit artist-author webpage
www.phyllisparun.com

For future notifications on new releases,
join author email list:
pbpstudio@yahoo.com

FiN

www.ingramcontent.com/pod-product-compliance
Lightning Source LLC
Chambersburg PA
CBHW052211090526
44584CB00019BA/3049